W9-BEZ-202

3 1668 04248 4219

CHILDREN 641.59 SMITHYMAN
    2006
Smithyman, Kathryn
Native North American foods
    and recipes
Central   08/18/2010

CENTRAL LIBRARY

NATIVE NATIONS · OF NORTH AMERICA ·

Native North American
FOODS and RECIPES

Kathryn Smithyman & Bobbie Kalman
Crabtree Publishing Company
www.crabtreebooks.com

FORT WORTH LIBRARY

Native North American Foods and Recipes

Dedicated by Kathryn Smithyman
To my small group: Lynne, Janine, Edmund, Lisa, Richard, and Steve

Editor-in-Chief
Bobbie Kalman

Writing team
Kathryn Smithyman
Bobbie Kalman

Substantive editor
Amanda Bishop

Editors
Molly Aloian
Robin Johnson
Kelley MacAulay

Design
Katherine Kantor

Production coordinator
Heather Fitzpatrick

Photo research
Crystal Foxton

Consultant
Patricia McCormack,
Associate Professor,
School of Native Studies,
University of Alberta

Special thanks to
Andrew Key, Jennifer Olarte, Sara Paton, Chantelle Styres, Tiffany Styres,
Sam Churchill and University Park Community Center

Illustrations
Barbara Bedell: back cover (maize), pages 10 (top), 12, 16 (top), 19, 21, 25, 28
Katherine Kantor: back cover (corn tortilla), pages 3 (pot and acorns),
    10 (bottom), 11 (acorns), 15, 17 (all except background)
Bonna Rouse: back cover (beans), pages 4 (map), 11 (all except acorns), 14
Margaret Amy Salter: back cover (all except beans, corn tortilla, and maize),
    title page (background), pages 3 (fish, flower, and basket), 4 (background),
    7, 9 (right), 13 (right), 17 (background), 22, 27 (squash)
Tiffany Wybouw: page 27 (cranberries)

Photographs and reproductions
Sherry Harrington: front cover
Sam Churchill: page 30 (top)
The Greenwich Workshop, Inc. Seymour, CT: © Howard Terpning:
    Old Country Buffet—The Feast (detail), page 23
Jack Paluh Arts, www.jackpaluh.com, 1-814-796-4400: page 8
Bobbie Kalman: pages 3 (people and top left), 7, 22, 30 (bottom)
© Permission of Lazare & Parker: pages 9 (left), 13 (left), 20, 24
Illustration by Gordon Miller: page 26
Nokomis: page 29
The Philbrook Museum of Art, Tulsa, Oklahoma: Charles Pushetonequa,
    Making Maple Syrup, 1951, 1951.15, watercolor: title page;
    Acee Blue Eagle, *Creek Women Cooking Fish*, 1950, 1950.10, watercolor: page 5
Smithsonian American Art Museum, Washington, DC/Art Resource, NY: page 16
© Craig Tennant: page 6
Other images by Circa: Art/Image Club Graphics, Comstock, Digital Vision,
    and Photodisc

Crabtree Publishing Company

www.crabtreebooks.com   1-800-387-7650

Copyright © **2006 CRABTREE PUBLISHING COMPANY.**
All rights reserved. No part of this publication may be
reproduced, stored in a retrieval system or be transmitted in
any form or by any means, electronic, mechanical, photocopying,
recording, or otherwise, without the prior written permission
of Crabtree Publishing Company. In Canada: We acknowledge
the financial support of the Government of Canada through
the Book Publishing Industry Development Program (BPIDP)
for our publishing activities.

Cataloging-in-Publication Data
Native North American foods and recipes / Kathryn Smithyman & Bobbie Kalman.
    p. cm. -- (Native nations of North America)
Includes index.
ISBN-13: 978-0-7787-0383-9 (rlb)
ISBN-10: 0-7787-0383-5 (rlb)
ISBN-13: 978-0-7787-0475-1 (pbk)
ISBN-10: 0-7787-0475-0 (pbk)
    1. Indian cookery--North America--Juvenile literature. 2. Indians of North America--
Food--Juvenile literature. I. Kalman, Bobbie. II. Title. III. Series.
    TX715.S6685 2005
    641.59'297--dc22

2005019989
LC

**Published in
the United States**
PMB16A
350 Fifth Ave.
Suite 3308
New York, NY
10118

**Published
in Canada**
616 Welland Ave.,
St. Catharines, Ontario,
Canada
L2M 5V6

**Published in the
United Kingdom**
73 Lime Walk
Headington
Oxford
OX3 7AD
United Kingdom

**Published
in Australia**
386 Mt. Alexander Rd.,
Ascot Vale (Melbourne)
VIC 3032

Contents

Native to North America

Native people lived in North America for thousands of years before Europeans arrived in the 1400s. Hundreds of thousands of Native people lived throughout North America. They belonged to many **nations**. A nation is a group of people who share languages, beliefs, and customs. Different nations lived in different **regions** of North America. **Anthropologists** now divide North America into ten regions. The regions are shown on the map below. They are the Arctic, the Subarctic, the Plateau, the Northwest Coast, California, the Great Basin, the Great Plains, the Southwest, the Southeast, and the Northeast.

Territories
Each nation had its own **territory**, or area of land in which its people lived, hunted, and gathered food. Some nations were made up of thousands of people, whereas others had fewer than a thousand members. The people of most nations lived in towns or villages, but they also traveled from place to place within their territories to find food. Some nations did not live in permanent locations but continually moved from place to place.

Foods from nature

The people of all nations valued their territories and the **natural resources** these lands contained. Everything the people needed for their survival came from the land and water in their territories. Each territory contained a variety of plants and animals. The people of most nations hunted, fished, and gathered plant foods from the forests, grasslands, lakes, and rivers. Nations that lived in deserts relied on desert plants and animals. Nations that lived near oceans hunted seals and other ocean mammals, caught many kinds of fish, and gathered shellfish.

Working together

Hunting, fishing, and gathering foods took a lot of time and effort. Native people knew where to find the resources they needed. They moved throughout their territories to find the animals and plant foods on which they relied. Hunters or gatherers often worked together to find enough food for their people. People sometimes worked together in small family groups to collect food and other resources. At other times, large groups of people gathered together to collect resources. Large gatherings were times for people to socialize and celebrate with one another.

People worked together to prepare the foods they ate. Each nation prepared fish and other foods in slightly different ways.

A variety of foods

As you read this book, you will discover that many of the foods in your local grocery stores were first gathered or grown by Native North Americans. Perhaps you eat some of these foods every day! Native people gathered a variety of fruits, vegetables, and other plant foods, including many kinds of berries and nuts, wild rice, potatoes, and prairie turnips.

Hundreds of recipes

Men were often responsible for hunting, but women also hunted, both on their own and in groups with men. Men sometimes prepared and cooked foods, especially when they were traveling. In most nations, however, women were responsible for gathering, farming, and cooking. Native women prepared the foods in a variety of ways. Although the recipes were not written down until later times, Native cooks created hundreds of dishes. Today, people all over the world continue to enjoy Native North American foods and recipes.

Native people gathered over 47 kinds of berries, including strawberries, blueberries, currants, and cherries, as shown above.

Try for yourself!

The recipes in this book use ingredients that Native North American people grew and used. Today, some Native people prepare certain foods using traditional methods and ingredients, but most add ingredients to their recipes that were not available to their **ancestors**. They also use modern appliances and cooking methods. The recipes in this book include non-traditional ingredients and cooking methods.

Safety first

It is important to be safe while you are cooking. Make sure there is an adult supervising while you prepare and cook the foods shown in this book. Before you begin, check the recipe for ingredients to which you are **allergic**. Be sure to read the labels of all packaged foods carefully. The list, below right, includes additional safety tips.

- Before handling foods, always wash and dry your hands. Also wash your hands thoroughly after handling raw eggs or meat.
- Wash all vegetables and fruits, even if you plan to peel them.
- Turn the handles of pots and pans away from the edges of the stove, so you do not accidentally bump into them and spill hot foods on yourself or on others.
- Always wear oven mitts when lifting foods into or out of an oven or when holding a pot on the stove.

Respecting nature

The people of all nations respected nature. Every day, they offered thanks for the plants and animals on which they depended for their survival. They showed their gratitude with prayers, songs, dances, and ceremonies.

Before and after hunting, Native people thanked the spirits of the animals for giving up their lives.

Little waste

Native people showed respect for nature by **conserving**, or not wasting, resources. Most Native hunters killed only the animals that they needed in order to survive.

Native people used all the parts of the animals they killed, even the parts they did not eat. They made tools, weapons, shelters, and clothing from animal bones and animal **hides**, or skins.

Food all year

Many foods were not available year round. People used their resources carefully to ensure they had food for the entire year. They ate some of the food and saved the rest. This **surplus**, or extra, food was **preserved** so it would not spoil. People ate preserved foods when fresh foods were not available. Some preserved foods were traded with other nations for different foods or goods. People often traded items that were available to them for meat from animals that did not live in their territories. Nations also traded goods or foods in exchange for berries, nuts, and other plant foods that did not grow in their territories.

Foods from fields and forests

For the people of some nations, certain foods they gathered from fields and forests were **staple** foods. Staple foods are important foods that are eaten nearly every day. Specific plants were also gathered and used as medicines. Some plants grew near where the people lived and were gathered as they were needed. Other plants grew only in particular parts of a territory, so people traveled to collect them. Some foods took several days or weeks to gather, so people set up temporary camps at the sites where the plants grew. Often, some people gathered foods while others prepared the foods to be transported back to their villages.

Berries had to be gathered as soon as they were ripe, or they would be eaten by birds, bears, coyotes, and other hungry animals.

Cultivating wild plants

For thousands of years, Native North Americans have **cultivated** certain plants. When people cultivate plants, they care for the plants to help them grow. Many nations cultivated plants in the areas where the plants grew naturally. Oak trees and berry bushes were two types of plants that people weeded and pruned so they would produce plenty of nuts and fruit.

Controlled fires
One way Native people kept wild plants, such as berry bushes and groups of nut trees, healthy was by setting them on fire. These **controlled fires** were set only in certain areas. The fires burned up old dried-out plants and made room for young plants to grow. Young plants produced more seeds, nuts, and fruits than did the older plants.

Prickly pear cacti
The prickly pear is a type of cactus that grows in the deserts of the Southwest region. It has flat stems called *nopales*. In spring, the cactus is covered with many flowers that become fruits called *tunas*. Both nopales and tunas were staple foods for people in the Southwest. After the spines covering the stems were removed, the nopales were served raw or were boiled. Tunas were crushed to make juice or jelly, or they were dried and added to other dishes. Prickly pear cacti contained a lot of water, so people in the region often cut open the cacti and drank the juices. People also used cacti to make medicines and **dyes**.

Acorns

Acorns are nuts that grow on oak trees. They were a staple food for most of the nations from the California region. Acorns had to be ground and then washed in order to **leach**, or remove from them, a bitter-tasting acid that they contained. After they were ground and leached, acorns were used to make foods such as breads, cakes, and soups.

Camas

Camas is an onionlike plant that was once plentiful throughout the Plateau region. Fields of camas grew in open grasslands. In summer, people used pointed digging sticks to dig up camas roots. They boiled the roots to make soup or baked them for long periods of time in underground pits. Baked camas sweetened stews and other foods. Camas roots were also dried and stored.

Maple sugar and wild rice

In the Northeast region, gatherers collected two important foods—sap and wild rice. Most nations gathered sap from maple trees. The sap was used to make maple sugar. People used maple sugar to flavor many kinds of foods. Wild rice was a staple food for many nations in the region. Both maple sugar and wild rice were also enjoyed by people in the neighboring Southeast and Great Plains regions, who offered their most valued trade items in exchange for these foods.

Collecting maple sap

In spring, when maple trees produced sap, people moved from their villages and set up temporary camps in the maple forests. Gatherers collected sap by making V-shaped cuts in the trees. They inserted hollow reeds or wooden spouts into the cuts and placed birchbark baskets beneath the spouts to collect the sap that dripped from the trees.

From sap to sugar

Women heated stones in a fire, then added them to the containers of sap. The hot stones caused the sap to boil, making a thick syrup. Some syrup was set aside for immediate use, but most was boiled until it became very thick. The thickened syrup was placed in long wooden **troughs** and stirred with wooden paddles until it cooled and turned to sugar. Most of the sap was made into sugar because sugar lasted for months and was easy to store.

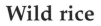

Wild rice

Wild rice is a type of grain that grows on tall stalks of grass along the shores of lakes, marshes, and ponds in the Northeast region. When the rice ripened in late summer, families set up camps near the shores. The people spent about six weeks gathering and preparing the wild rice.

Native people gathered all the wild rice they needed but always left behind enough rice to feed the birds and to ensure that there would be another harvest the following year.

Gathering the rice

To gather the rice, two people worked together in a canoe. One person stood in the back of the canoe and used a long pole to steer through the dense stalks. The other person pulled the stalks over the canoe and hit them with wooden sticks to knock the grains of rice off the plants. When the canoe was full, the people returned to shore so others could prepare the rice for eating.

Preparing the rice

Native people prepared wild rice by laying it on sheets of birch bark to dry in the sun. The rice was sometimes **parched**, or heated over an open fire. To remove the rice **husks**, or outer coverings, people placed the rice in a shallow pit lined with birch bark and walked or danced on it. Next, the rice was **winnowed**, or placed in a shallow tray and tossed in the air. As it was winnowed, the husks blew away in the wind. The rice was stored in birchbark containers or in bags made from animal skins.

13

Cultivating crops

People from many nations were farmers. They planted and grew food **crops**, including sunflowers, corn, beans, squash, chilies, peanuts, and pumpkins. They cultivated these crops in fields located near their towns and villages. Native people planted crops to have reliable food sources. Large fields of crops provided enough food to last everyone in a town or village from one **growing season** to the next. Some crops grew only in one region. For example, chilies grew only in the Southwest region. Other crops, such as corn, grew well in several regions.

Domesticated plants

Nearly half of the foods in the world today come from plants that were **domesticated** by Native people in North America and South America. To domesticate plants means to change them to make them more suitable for people. Native farmers domesticated plants over time by **sowing** seeds only from wild plants that had the qualities they wanted. Eventually, the domesticated plants became different than the wild plants. Native farmers domesticated as many as 40 different kinds of plants, which they used for foods and medicines.

The three sisters

For nations in the Southwest, Southeast, and Northeast regions, as well as in the eastern half of the Great Plains region, corn, beans, and squash were staple foods. Many stews included all three of these foods. Eaten together, these foods make up a healthy meal. In the Northeast region, women called crops of corn, beans, and squash the "three sisters." The name "sisters" refers to the plants and also to the spirits of the plants. These crops were planted together because they helped one another grow. The tall corn stalks provided support for the bean plants, which climbed up around the corn stalks. Squash grew between the corn stalks. The large leaves of the squash plants shaded the ground, kept it moist, and prevented weeds from growing.

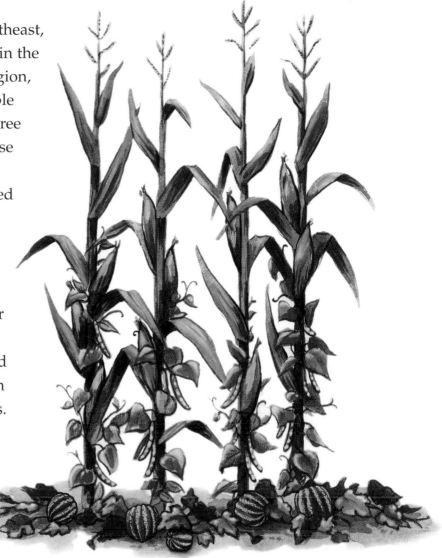

Sunflowers

Sunflowers were among the first crops domesticated by Native people in North America. They were grown in most regions. In autumn, the heads of ripe sunflowers were broken off, dried, and beaten with sticks to release the seeds. Sunflower seeds could be eaten raw or used to make oil or butter. The seeds were also **roasted** and ground into **meal** for making bread. Roasted seeds could be **brewed** to make a coffeelike drink. The Hopi people of the Southwest region made yellow dye from sunflower petals and purple dye from sunflower seeds.

15

A valued crop

Corn was one of the most valued foods grown by Native North American farmers. The people who lived in the Southwest and Southeast regions were the first people in North America to grow corn. Thousands of years ago, they acquired seeds and learned how to grow corn from their neighbors in the **Valley of Mexico**. Before long, the nations living in the Southwest and Southeast regions began trading their corn seeds and crops with nations that lived in other regions of North America.

People in the Southwest region grew many types of corn, including yellow corn, white corn, blue corn, and red corn.

Easy to grow

The Southwest region is dry, and there are few rivers. Despite the dry weather, farmers in the Southwest region developed varieties of corn that grew successfully there. They also developed **irrigation systems**, or ways of getting river water to the crops. Farmers in other regions also developed varieties of corn that suited their own lands and **climates**. As a result, farmers from different regions grew many different types of corn.

Preparing corn

Women prepared and cooked corn in many ways. They added kernels of fresh corn to meat and vegetable stews in order to sweeten them. They also dried kernels of corn in the sun to preserve them. Dried kernels were often popped over a fire to make popcorn or were pounded into coarse flour. The flour, called **cornmeal**, was used to make breads. People also mixed cornmeal with beans and other vegetables to make pancakes and puddings.

Maple popcorn balls

Preparation time: 5 minutes
Cooking time: 15 minutes
Servings: 8

Equipment: measuring cup and spoons, heavy saucepan, long-handled spoon, large heat-proof bowl, greased baking sheet
Ingredients:
1 large bag of plain popped popcorn
1 cup (250 ml) maple syrup
2 teaspoons (10 ml) butter

Method:
1. Pour popcorn into a bowl.
2. Heat the syrup and the butter in a saucepan over medium-high heat. Stir constantly using a long-handled spoon until the mixture thickens.
3. Remove the mixture from the heat and pour it over the popcorn.
4. When the mixture is cool enough, use your hands to blend the syrup mixture with the popcorn.
5. Shape the popcorn into balls and place them on a greased baking sheet.
6. Leave the popcorn balls on the sheet to cool completely before eating them.

In the Southwest region, corn was ground into flour and used to make flat, round tortillas.

Hunting animals for meat

The people of most nations hunted animals for meat. Native hunters caught small animals, such as rabbits, raccoons, and squirrels, using nets or **snares**. Some hunted large animals, such as bears, elks, deer, and antelopes, using snares, traps, bows and arrows, and spears. Bison were hunted in every region in which the animals roamed, including the Subarctic, Plateau, Great Basin, Great Plains, and Northeast regions.

Hunting camps

Hunters knew that in some seasons, certain species of animals gathered together. The hunters traveled to these areas and set up temporary camps. Often, after successful hunts, families prepared and preserved the meat at the camps. If hunters were hunting large animals, they moved the camps to the places where the animals had been killed.

Native people also hunted land birds, such as turkeys, and water birds, such as ducks. They gathered and ate bird eggs, too.

Bison hunters

Before Europeans arrived in North America, most Native nations in the Great Plains region lived in villages that were close to rivers. By living near water, people could grow crops such as corn and melons. Hunters made short trips to hunt bison and other animals. They caught bison by **herding**, or leading, the animals to places where they were trapped. Some bison hunters used large stones to create V-shaped pathways, which led toward cliffs. Hunters wore wolf skins over their heads and shoulders to frighten the bison. The scared animals ran through the narrowing pathways and over the cliffs to their deaths. Native people then collected the bison from below the cliffs and prepared them for eating. The people of other nations herded bison into fenced-in areas of land and killed the bison there.

Hunting with horses

Soon after Europeans brought horses to North America, the hunters of the Great Plains region learned how to tame and ride the horses. Great Plains hunters became skilled at chasing and hunting bison on horseback. People also used horses to transport their homes and supplies as they followed herds of bison from place to place. Some nations followed the herds in certain seasons and returned to their villages and farms for the rest of the year. Other nations abandoned farming as a way of life, left their villages, and followed herds of bison year round.

Delicious meat
Women from the Great Plains region made hearty stews from bison meat. They added herbs, root vegetables, and berries to the stews. They dried some bison meat and made it into hard strips called **jerky**. Jerky could be kept for long periods of time and was an excellent food to eat while traveling.

Catching fish and other foods

Many nations lived near bodies of water. Nations that lived along the coasts of North America caught whales, seals, and many kinds of fish in the Arctic, Atlantic, and Pacific oceans. Most **inland** nations fished in the lakes, rivers, and streams in or around their territories. These people caught many kinds of fish, including trout, sturgeon, perch, bass, and pickerel. They used harpoons, spears, hooks and lines, nets, and **weirs** to catch fish. Weirs are fences placed in water to trap fish. Some people fished from boats or kayaks, as shown left, whereas others fished from shore. Native fishers knew the best fishing locations and returned to them year after year.

Hunting arctic animals

Plant foods were scarce in the Arctic region, so the nations that lived there survived by hunting caribou, polar bears, whales, seals, walruses, and sea lions. These animals provided people with meat and **blubber**, or animal fat. They ate the meat and blubber and also burned the blubber as fuel. In addition to using the meat and blubber, people of the Arctic made clothing and shelters from animal furs and skins and created tools from animal bones.

Hunters from the Arctic region used harpoons to hunt ocean animals, such as whales and seals.

Salmon

Most of the nations that lived along coasts caught salmon, but it was highly valued among nations in the Northwest Coast region. At the beginning of every **salmon run**, most salmon fishers held ceremonies to thank the spirits of the salmon. A salmon run took place during a few weeks each year, when millions of salmon swam upstream from oceans into rivers to lay eggs. As the fish swam upstream, Native fishers caught large numbers of them with spears, nets, or weirs. In the Northwest Coast region, people also gathered salmon eggs, which they thought of as a **delicacy**, or special food.

Salmon bake

Preparation time: 15 minutes
Cooking time: 20 minutes
Servings: 2

Equipment: sharp knife, cutting board, measuring spoons, baking sheet or shallow baking dish, fork

Ingredients:

1 teaspoon (5 ml) oil
1 pound (455 g) salmon fillet, cut in half
2 small tomatoes, chopped
5 green onions, chopped
$\frac{1}{4}$ teaspoon (2 g) salt
$\frac{1}{4}$ teaspoon (2 g) pepper

Method:

1. Preheat oven to 350° F (175° C).
2. Spread oil over a baking sheet or baking dish, then place the salmon fillets on it. Fold under the thin outer edges of the fillets, so they do not burn or dry out as they cook.
3. Cover the salmon with the tomatoes and green onions. Season with salt and pepper.
4. Cook the salmon uncovered for about 30 minutes. The salmon is ready when it flakes apart easily with a fork.

People who lived along coasts gathered shellfish, including abalones, mussels, barnacles, scallops, and clams. This woman from the Northwest Coast region is digging up clams. Clams were a staple food for many nations.

21

Cooking

Native people cooked a wide variety of foods in water. The people of many nations prepared delicious soups and stews by boiling vegetables and then adding meats, nuts, and berries to the pots. Many cooks boiled soups over fires. Other cooks heated stones in fires and then added them to their cooking pots to make the soups hot.

Roasting and baking

In regions where water was scarce, people often roasted vegetables and other foods instead of cooking them in water. Foods could be roasted over open fires or baked in pits that were lined with hot coals or ashes. People sometimes wrapped foods in wet leaves before putting them in the pits. The leaves added flavor as the foods roasted. Many kinds of bulbs, **tubers**, and other roots were roasted in hot ashes. They were eaten or added to soups or stews. Some foods were roasted and then ground into flour.

Hearty soup

Preparation time: 30 minutes
Cooking time: 45 minutes
Servings: 6

Equipment: sharp knife, cutting board, measuring cups and spoons, large saucepan with a lid, long-handled spoon

Ingredients:
2 leeks or 1 onion
2 celery stalks or 1 green pepper
6 carrots or 4 parsnips
1 cup corn kernels
2 tablespoons (30 ml) cooking oil
4 cups (1 liter) water
one 28-ounce (796 ml) can stewed tomatoes
2 cups (500 ml) vegetable or chicken broth
one 19-ounce (540 ml) can mixed beans
salt and pepper

Method:
1. Wash the vegetables. (Leeks are very sandy and should be washed well.)
2. On a cutting board, cut up the leeks or onion into small pieces. Chop the celery and carrots, as well.
3. Pour the oil into a large saucepan. Add the carrots, leeks, and celery. Cover the pan with a lid and cook the vegetables over low heat for five minutes, stirring occasionally with a long-handled spoon.
4. Add the water, tomatoes, and broth. Bring the soup to a boil. Reduce the heat and **simmer** for about 30 minutes, or until the vegetables are tender.
5. Add the corn and the mixed beans. Season the soup with salt and pepper. Simmer for another ten minutes.

Most meals were plentiful enough to feed everyone in a village or camp.

Preserving and storing foods

Many foods were available only at certain times of the year, so people developed ways of preserving and storing the foods they needed. Many families relied on preserved foods during the months when fresh foods were not available.

Dried foods

One way people preserved foods was by drying them. They air-dried a variety of foods, including meats, fish, corn, beans, nuts, seeds, and green plants. To dry these foods, people placed them on the roofs of their houses or hung them on racks in the sun. Native women also dried berries, which they used throughout the year to flavor dishes. Some berries, such as cranberries, were dried whole. Other berries were mashed before they were dried. Mashed berries stuck together and formed flat sheets, which could then be dried.

Many people dried foods by hanging them inside their homes, which contained cooking fires.

Smoked foods

When the weather was not hot or sunny enough to air-dry foods, people dried foods over fires using a process called **smoking**. Smoking added flavor to meats, fish, and vegetables. Smoking foods also kept insects away from the foods as they were drying. Before smoking meat or fish, the pieces were cut into thin strips so that they would dry completely.

Safe storage

It was important to store foods in places that kept them dry and away from hungry animals. Preserved foods were stored in animal skins and in sealed containers made of birch bark, clay, or wood. The people of many nations dug pits in the ground in which they stored containers of preserved foods, as shown on page 24. Some nations built storage houses for corn and other foods.

Pemmican

The people of many nations made **pemmican**, which is a combination of dried meat, fat, nuts, and berries. Pemmican was made from bison, deer, rabbit, squirrel, or other meat. The people laid dried meat on a flat surface and pounded it until it turned into powder or flakes. They added melted fat and sometimes added berries and nuts to the powdered meat. Pemmican could be stored for months. It was a perfect food to eat while traveling because people could eat pemmican without having to stop and cook it.

Making meal

Many dried foods were ground into meal or flour to make them easier to store and to use. The women of all nations made dough using meal and flour. Many kinds of nuts and seeds were first dried and then ground into meal. People in the California region pounded dried acorns into flour using heavy rocks. Those who grew sunflowers used rounded stones called *manos* to grind the seeds into meal. They ground the seeds on flat stones called *metates*.

In the Southwest region, women made cornmeal by using manos and metates to crush dried corn kernels, as shown above. In the Northeast region, women placed kernels in hollowed logs and pounded them with logs or carved sticks.

Food and celebrations

Food was, and continues to be, an important part of **hospitality** among Native communities. Guests and travelers were fed immediately when they arrived at a town or village, and the best foods were prepared in their honor. It was considered polite for visitors to eat everything offered to them. Native people believed that foods were gifts from the Creator. They held seasonal celebrations to honor the Creator and the spirits. Most celebrations included ceremonies, **rituals**, feasts, dancing, and storytelling. Many celebrations were centered around successful hunts, the changing seasons, and the planting or harvesting of crops. Native people continue to participate in these celebrations today. Feasts are still part of the celebrations.

*People of the Northwest Coast region held many ceremonies. One important ceremony was a gift-giving ceremony called a **potlatch**. A potlatch gave the host an opportunity to display his wealth and generosity by treating guests to food, singing, and dancing.*

26

The pilgrims arrive

In 1621, a group of Europeans, called the Pilgrims, landed in present-day Plymouth, Massachusetts. They settled in Wampanoag territory in the Northeast region. The leader of the Wampanoag nation was called Massasoit. Massasoit agreed to trade with the Pilgrims. The Pilgrims learned a lot about fishing, hunting, and gathering from the Wampanoag people.

A feast of thanksgiving

In the autumn of 1621, the Pilgrims hosted a trade negotiation with the Wampanoag, which was followed by a feast. As was his custom, Massasoit arrived with a large group of his people and plenty of food. The Wampanoag brought deer meat, roast duck, roast goose, wild turkey, corn bread, maple sugar, berries, corn, squash, and pumpkins. This feast was the first harvest celebration for the Pilgrims. To the Wampanoag, however, it was only one of the several feasts of thanksgiving they celebrated each year. Many people still call the feast shared by the Pilgrims and the Wampanoag the "first Thanksgiving." To this day, thousands of North Americans eat turkey, pumpkin, and cranberries as "traditional" Thanksgiving foods.

Acorn squash stuffed with cranberries

Preparation time: 25 minutes
Cooking time: 60 minutes
Servings: 4

Equipment: large sharp knife, spoon, measuring cups and spoons, large baking dish, medium mixing bowl, grater
Ingredients:
4 small acorn squash
2 cups (500 ml) whole fresh
    or frozen cranberries
½ cup (125 ml) applesauce
½ teaspoon (2 ml) grated orange peel
½ cup (125 ml) maple syrup

Method:
1. Preheat oven to 350° F (175° C).
2. Ask an adult to cut each squash in half. Using a spoon, scoop out the seeds and discard them.
3. Place the eight halves into a baking dish with the skin sides up. Bake for 35 minutes.
4. Remove the squash from the oven and set aside to cool.
5. In a medium mixing bowl, combine the cranberries, applesauce, orange peel, and maple syrup.
6. Turn the cooled squash halves skin-side down and fill them with the cranberry mixture.
7. Return the filled squash halves to the oven and bake for another 25-30 minutes.
8. Remove the squash from the oven and serve immediately.

Exchanging foods

Few of the Europeans who first arrived in North America would have survived without the help of Native Americans. Europeans discovered that some of the foods they had grown in Europe did not grow well in North America. They soon realized, however, that Native crops, such as corn, grew well and fed many people. European settlers sometimes traded with Native people in order to get these foods. Some settlers even stole foods from Native farms. The settlers soon started cooking Native foods. They boiled corn and beans together to make **succotash**.

They also made **hominy**, **grits**, and corn bread. The settlers added fruits such as cranberries to their dishes. They also enjoyed the taste of maple sugar and maple syrup. Over time, the settlers learned Native methods of gathering foods, such as maple sap. They also learned how to hunt and fish using Native techniques.

As modern equipment became available, the settlers used it to gather sap. The Native method of gathering sap and turning it into maple syrup and maple sugar is still used today, however.

New ingredients

Through trade, the settlers introduced foods, such as wheat flour and sugar, to Native people. Some foods, such as potatoes, were foods that Europeans had acquired through trade with Native people in South America! Settlers also introduced animals, such as pigs and cows, to Native people. Settlers raised these animals and used the meat in their cooking. The settlers used cheese, milk, and other dairy products in their recipes, which the people of most Native nations had never before used. In some regions, Native cooks added these and other new ingredients to their traditional recipes. One of the dishes that some nations developed using these ingredients was called "fry bread" by some nations and "bannock" by others. People from each nation made fry bread or bannock slightly differently, but most made the dough using flour, salt, and baking powder. People shaped the dough into disks and fried it in oil until it was brown and crispy.

The painting shown above is by a Native artist called Nokomis. It shows the artist and her mother making bannock.

Changing ways of life
As more and more non-Native people settled in North America, many nations were forced from their territories. When the governments of the United States and Canada were formed, they **prohibited**, or forbade, Native people from hunting, gathering foods, or farming in their traditional ways. Native people were forced to change their ways of life. They cooked and ate the foods that were available to them. As a result, the foods and recipes used by Native North Americans became similar to the foods and recipes used by most other North Americans.

Nations today

Today, Native people have lifestyles that are similar to the lifestyles of other Americans and Canadians. Some are successful farmers and ranchers. Others are doctors, police officers, or hold other jobs. They buy most, or all, of their food in grocery stores. At the same time, many Native people continue to practice the traditions, languages, and ceremonies of their nations. The people of most nations hold the same annual celebrations that their people have always held. Traditional foods are part of these celebrations.

A salmon bake is included in the annual celebrations of Native people from the Northwest Coast region.

Bean salad

Preparation time: 20 minutes plus refrigeration time of 30 minutes
Servings: 4

Equipment: colander, sharp knife, cutting board, measuring cups and spoons, peeler, grater, large bowl, small bowl, spoon, whisk
Ingredients:
one 19-ounce (540 ml) can of mixed beans
$^1/_2$ cup (125 ml) chopped cucumber
1 carrot, peeled and grated
1 handful of chopped fresh parsley
1 celery stalk, sliced
$^1/_4$ cup (50 ml) red onion, diced
3 tablespoons (45 ml) olive oil
2 teaspoons (10 ml) hot sauce
pinch of black pepper

Method:
1. Place the beans in a colander and rinse them under running water until there is no foam.
2. Wash all the vegetables.
3. On the cutting board, chop the cucumber, celery, parsley, and onion.
4. Peel the carrot and then grate it.
5. In a large bowl and using a spoon, mix the beans, cucumber, carrot, parsley, celery, and onion.
6. In a small bowl, whisk together the olive oil, hot sauce, and black pepper to make a dressing. Pour the dressing over the salad ingredients in the large bowl and stir until they are coated with the dressing.
7. Refrigerate the salad for 30 minutes. Stir again before serving.

Pumpkin bread

Preparation time: 25 minutes
Cooking time: 50 minutes
Servings: 8

Equipment: greased loaf pan, 2 large mixing bowls, measuring cups and spoons, hand mixer, fork, toothpick
Ingredients:
1 ½ cups (375 ml) sugar
½ cup (125 ml) vegetable oil
1 cup (250 ml) canned pure pumpkin
2 eggs
⅓ cup (75 ml) water
¾ cup (175 ml) whole-wheat flour
1 ¼ cup (300 ml) white flour
1 teaspoon (5 ml) baking soda
1 teaspoon (5 ml) salt
¼ teaspoon (1.25 ml) baking powder
½ cup (125 ml) raisins or dried apples
   or dried cranberries or walnut pieces
2 teaspoons (10 ml) of allspice or
   pumpkin pie spice

Method:
1. Preheat oven to 300° F (150° C).
2. In one bowl, mix together the sugar, oil, pumpkin, eggs, and water using a hand mixer.
3. In another bowl, mix the whole-wheat flour, white flour, baking soda, salt, and baking powder using a fork.
4. Add the flour mixture to the pumpkin mixture and stir with the fork until moistened. Add fruit or nuts, if desired. Stir.
5. Pour the batter into a loaf pan.
6. Bake for one hour, or until a toothpick inserted into the middle of the bread comes out clean.
7. Cool the bread before slicing it.

Wild rice salad

Preparation time: 20 minutes plus refrigeration time of 30 minutes
Cooking time: 50 minutes
Servings: 6

Equipment: fork, measuring cups and spoons, saucepan with a lid, colander, frying pan, knife, cutting board, whisk, large bowl, small bowl
Ingredients:
1 cup (250 ml) brown and wild rice
2 cups (500 ml) water
½ red pepper, sliced
¼ cup (60 ml) red onion, sliced
1 tomato, diced
½ cup (125 ml) cranraisins
¼ cup (60 ml) olive oil
juice of ½ lemon
a dash of hot sauce
a pinch of salt

Method:
1. In a colander, rinse the rice under cold water. Place the rice and the four cups of water into a saucepan. Bring to a boil. Place the lid on the saucepan and reduce the heat to medium-low for 40 minutes. Remove from the heat and stir the rice with a fork.
2. Using one teaspoon of the olive oil, **sauté** the peppers and onion in a frying pan for about three minutes.
3. Combine the vegetables and rice in a large bowl. Add the cranraisins.
4. In a small bowl, whisk together the remaining olive oil, lemon juice, hot sauce, and salt to make a dressing. Pour the dressing over the salad.
5. Stir the salad. Refrigerate salad for 30 minutes or overnight before serving.

Glossary

Note: Boldfaced words that are defined in the book may not appear in the glossary.

allergic Describing an adverse reaction brought about by a food or other cause

ancestor An ancient relative from whom someone is descended

anthropologist A person who studies people, especially the development of cultures

brew To make by soaking in boiling water

climate The weather conditions in an area in general or over a long period of time

dye A natural substance used to add color to or change the color of an object

elder An older person who is respected for his or her wisdom

growing season The part of the year during which rainfall and temperature allow plants to grow

herd To lead animals, such as bison or sheep

hominy Coarsely ground corn kernels

hospitality The friendly and generous treatment of guests, visitors, or strangers

grits A dish of coarsely ground corn kernels boiled with water or milk

inland Areas of land that are not located near coasts

meal A coarse powder made by grinding seeds or grains

natural resources The useful materials found in nature, such as wood

preserve To prepare foods so they do not spoil

ritual A ceremony consisting of a series of actions performed in a certain order

roast To cook food by heating for a long time in an oven or over a fire

sauté To cook food in a pan using a small amount of butter or oil

simmer To cook food in liquid so that it heats without boiling

smoking To preserve meat by drying it over smoky coals or a smoky fire

snare A device, usually consisting of a noose, for capturing birds or other small animals

sow To scatter seeds over land

succotash A cooked dish of kernels of corn mixed with beans

trough A boxlike container that is long, narrow, and open at the top

tuber A thick, underground part of a stem

Valley of Mexico A valley in ancient Mexico that was home to many Native nations

Index

1 2 3 4 5 6 7 8 9 0   Printed in the U.S.A.   4 3 2 1 0 9 8 7 6 5